"Out of the Nest"

The Handbook for New Adults

By
Annette M King
&
Daniel Hardt

A quick read of good advice for a big world filled with things you don't know that you don't know.

Note to the folks;
If your intention is to read this book before giving it to the young adult in your life who may need it, bravo! We applaud you! It is always more effective when everyone is on the same page and aware of the information exchanged. It may even lead to further curiosity and a chance for you to share more insight with your now adult child. Hopefully we hit all the highlights that your person will need to hear about *and then some!* If you feel anything in this handbook is inappropriate and doesn't apply to your particular person, even better.

Maybe they will not ever need to hear the advice about drinking and unprotected sex, but if they ever do or if they have a friend who does, they will have somewhere to draw from.

Don't censor the wisdom out of fear for the unknown. Let them fly with one more tool in their belt and trust them to learn when, if and how to use it. We got this!

Congratulations! If you bought this book for yourself, you are more adult than the majority of young people your age. If someone bought it for you, then congratulations! Someone loves you enough to arm your future with this tool to help guide you into adulthood.
Either way, you will be a few steps ahead of the crowd for reading this handbook, and our hope is that this wisdom will help you avoid learning some rough lessons the hard way.
I am Annette King. I am a wildlife rehabilitator. (keep reading. That's not my qualification here) I have spent 20 years running a program through the District Attorney's office in my community where people with minor legal charges can work off their time at my wildlife rescue facility rather than spending it in jail. The majority of our hundreds of assignees over the years have been young people, learning the hard way that adulting isn't easy and that a brief moment in time of a poor choice can haunt them a lifetime and cost tens of

thousands of dollars and their hard won freedom. I tell them all;

"The good thing about stupid is you can recover from it. Tragedy you can't."

We are sharing with you the little bits and pieces of life skill wisdom that most young people lack right out of the nest, which can save you a whole lot of struggle and make your transition to independence far less challenging. We have both said all of these things and more to the young people in our lives that we guide through their day to day challenges and pitfalls. Life is a journey without a road map. You are responsible for finding your way through it now. We want to give you some direction to help you navigate the unknown and mature as unscathed as possible. You will make mistakes, but here are some that maybe you can avoid for having read this handbook.

My husband, Dan Hardt, has a degree in community counseling. He is brilliant with advising young people, especially pre adults. He does not use his insight to earn a living but is there for anyone who needs him and is one of the most understanding and compassionate people I have ever met. His insight into the human condition is remarkable. I am the writer in the family, but he is "Dan the Man" and I have tapped his wisdom to enhance this handbook for you. Not a word will be published that he does not agree with so relax. You are in the hands of one professional and one who has spent a lifetime helping young people work through their problems. Enjoy learning to navigate your new world and please, by all means, *READ IT!* Having this book does not help you. Reading it, comprehending it and practicing its advice will help you. Hopefully your parents did their job well, but if they (or you) missed anything important, you will likely find it here. *You're welcome!*

Chapter 1
"YOU ARE FREE! (ish)"

Yes, yes you are. After eighteen or more years, you have finally crossed over into adulthood. Hopefully you have under your belt (or are soon to have) your hard won (by you and your parents) survival tools;

An education
Future goals
Morals
Ethics
A vehicle
A job
A roof over your head
Reliable friends
Support of family
Common sense

The last item "common sense" is probably the most important, but not all of us launch from the nest with an abundance, if any. As a matter of fact, some people are born with the gift of common sense while others have to earn it the hard way. Life experience will eventually create common sense, but this handbook is going to give you yet another tool to earn your "adulting" wings.

Your parents have spent eighteen plus years raising you. The day you were born their lives changed forever. They no longer came first in their own lives. You became the center of their world. Hopefully you are fortunate enough to have felt this way growing up, but if not, know that you are probably stronger for it though you may not realize it now. Those survival skills that come from being a neglected child will take you far in life, so no regrets okay? You can build your own support system now. It is all up to you. Be the person you need to count on in life and succeed in spite of your personal history. There are statistics that say you will struggle to manage your life. Don't become a statistic!

For those of you who were fortunate enough to be reading this and your mental checklist is saying *"I know that, I got that, that's a no brainer, yep I know that"* AWESOME!! You are well prepared for your journey into the future! Your wisdom to launch from the nest is intact and your parents should be applauded for their efforts in preparing you! You may find that you don't need this handbook after you read it, so pass it on to someone who may be struggling. You can now be a mentor for others and help them transition into adulthood.

Regardless of how prepared you are, your future lies ahead of you like an untamed mysterious wilderness of choices. You do not yet know that living at home and being parented was the easy part. You do not yet realize that freedom has a price. Your life will now be only what you make of it and your choices will teach you lessons both ways. From those lessons you will build your common sense. You will likely lose money, friends, jobs and respect along the way and you will suffer your own consequences on a regular basis. Our goal with this handbook is to give you some seeds to work with so that when you make a choice, you have something to guide you. Maybe you will avoid some of the consequences early, and many of the innocent but monumental mistakes we make that haunt us our entire lives will be avoided.

First things first;

CHAPTER 2
"Responsibility. Take some."

Here is a short list of things you may *think* you want now that you are on your own and technically an adult, but you really need to think again and consider *carefully*. This is a list of things that may backfire on you if you do not have the common sense to realize the disaster that may follow. We are speaking from experience here, and this wisdom will save you a ton of struggle.

DO NOT GET A PET- At this point, you are learning to take care of yourself. Why drag another life into the unsure and unknown. You just achieved freedom, and caring for an animal, like a child, is a full time obligation of time as well as money. You need to focus on yourself right now. Animal friends can wait until you are stable. Give yourself a chance to adjust to being on your own. The feeling of being alone and needing another life in your space will pass as you meet new people, obligate yourself to new activities and a pet might become a burden for you. If you still feel this way later, start with a goldfish. If you can't take proper care of a goldfish, don't even *think* about a dog or cat! ☺

DO NOT MOVE YOUR RELATIONSHIP IN WITH YOU- Can be far worse an outcome than getting a pet. Two people trying to figure out how to take care of themselves and maintaining a love interest commitment will most likely lead to disaster. Allow your independence to be a way to build on the relationship rather than commit to one by creating a family unit right off the bat. You may find that independence and maturity changes who you are and what you want in a partner, and they might not respond to you the same way as a responsible adult as they did when life was all taken care of. Get a reliable roommate who has a job if you need someone to share space with, and hold off on playing house for now. Take it slow. You are just now learning to fly. It's far too early to take on passengers.

LET THE PARTY HOUSE DREAM GO- Unless you are looking forward to cleaning trash, vomit, urine and other mysterious substances off your furniture and floors, feeding total strangers your hard earned food and being liable for everyone who walks out the door afterward, realize that part of being an adult is being responsible for what goes on under your roof. If this is on your agenda, be prepared to face a day when *'the fecal matter hits the rotary oscillator'* and it all comes to a screeching halt. You will be lucky if it doesn't include jail time or eviction. You cannot function at your full capacity in chaos. Though it might be fun to be an independent social station, sooner or later the fun wears off for you and no one will care. *Do not start anything you may not want to continue.* People may love you for being party central, but they will hate you when you become *the warden*. All the free beer and pizza in the world does not buy you friends. Its buys you *leaches*.

DO NOT BITE THE HAND THAT FEEDS YOU- If your parents or family are still lending support, this is not the time to show your independence and disregard rules, conditions, requests, invitations or curfews. Those hand outs are no longer an obligation. You are technically an adult and they can drop you like the sponge that you are any time they wish. As a parent, they have the need to make sure you are growing into a responsible adult, and they will lend support so long as they see that their support is helping you reach that goal. If you make poor choices and they feel that their support is enabling you in the wrong direction, they may choose the "tough love" route which is to drop you on your rear and let you figure it all out the hard way, which will send you directly back to them begging for another chance with your new found respect and appreciation for their support, willing to do things their way this time. Unfortunately you will have by then exhausted their resources and trust and the next round of support will be far more conditional and restrained. Trust me here; Preserve the first round and take advantage. Check in regularly, show up to family events, remember birthdays and Mother's/Father's Day. Keep track of your spending. Respect boundaries, curfews and limits. Don't be disrespectful and show appreciation for anything they do because at the end of this journey, they will be the *only* ones who *truly* care about you and what you need to survive in life. Your family will help you even when it creates problems for them to do so, and they are likely the only ones who ever will.

DO NOT RISK A PREGNANCY- Whether you are male or female, it doesn't matter. You are not yet ready to be a parent. Once you have a child, your life instantly becomes a journey on their behalf. What you want and what you need to be happy in the world is no longer your goals to have. What *they* need becomes your priority for the next *eighteen years minimum*. Your parents are not here to raise your children. They have raised their own. They deserve a break and shouldn't be expected to give up decades of freedom because you are careless and bring a child into this world before you are ready. Yes, you are technically an adult, but why in the world would you want to give up your freedom so soon? You *just* achieved your freedom. You are just now learning to spread your wings and fly from the nest. Having children chains you back to the nest and your nest at this point won't be nearly as awesome as you will want it to be. Face it, your nest would suck right now. Being a parent *does not* make you an adult. It makes you a parent. Live in your own sucky nest on your own for a while until you can build a better one worthy of a family, and know that your friends who are now having children this early are really *scared to death*.

DO NOT RISK A PREGNANCY WITH SOMEONE YOU DO NOT WANT TO SHARE YOUR LIFE WITH- If you didn't pay attention to the previous part, *LISTEN TO ME NOW*. There is a worse fate than being strapped with a child too soon in life. It is being a co-parent with someone who hates your guts. The bad news is that you have to do this for up to eighteen years. The good news is you only have to do this for up to eighteen years.

Selecting a partner to produce little people with should never be taken lightly or treated casually. You are tying yourself to this person and their family, and their friends, and their lifestyle and choices for what will seem like an eternity, and it just might be for the rest of your life. If you have a child with someone, there will never be a day when they will not have an opinion of you. For the years that the child is a child, you will share *everything* with them. Your money, your whereabouts and the person who means the most in the world to you; *your child*. IF the relationship is strong enough and you both suddenly materialize into responsible, self-sacrificing adults, the journey of raising a child will still be a struggle, and you will still both be giving up your own dreams, goals and freedom to ensure the person you created has all they need to thrive, but the chances of this "family" created before its time making it long term is *slim*. My best advice to you is to take a long, hard, serious look at the person you choose to have sex with, imagine them hating your guts one day and imagine having to hand them your most precious beloved child half of your life (*given the judge awards joint custody*), and having no control over anything when they drive away, and your life being an open book for them to review and criticize (*possibly in a court*) any time they feel the need for your attention or question your parenting methods. You will shell out thousands of dollars to battle for your child and no, you don't have to do anything wrong to be taken to court. Court will become part of your life and you will battle with feelings of giving up just to stop the madness, but you will know this fight is for the love of your child and you will stand strong and sacrifice all of your goals and dreams to save that relationship so that your child knows that you love and want them…. Then grab the condoms or opt to abstain. It's so not worth it to take the risk! Being a parent is a beautiful thing *when and if* you are ready. Some people are *never* ready. And yes, those people should possibly never have children! You will meet many of them along your journey and see that I am right on. The news is loaded with stories of people who should never have reproduced. Many of them began just as you are now, and the loss of all their hopes and dreams and the pressure of too soon responsibilities sent them down paths of self-destruction and drug the kids along for the demented ride.

I have nothing against having children, but I am opposed to *children having children*. It is *hard* to do it right, even when you are prepared, and you will need lots of help to establish a life where you can be a good parent. There are far too many grandparents raising children when they should be reaping the rewards of their retirement from parenting, but instead they are providing for little people and hoping they live long enough to keep their grandchildren safe from harm.

It is not fair, and though there are plenty of stories of young couples successfully having a family and making it decades together, ask them what they gave up. They all have a story of sacrifice.

If you want to have children someday, set your goals for career, make a checklist of everything you want to accomplish before you become a parent and do your best to stick to it. Casual sex creates children all the time. My daughter, whom I love more than anyone else on the planet and wouldn't trade for anything, was a result of a drunken party when I was twenty. I barely knew the guy. I was enlisted in the US Air Force, headed to basic training when I found out I was pregnant. Instead I got married, bought a house, worked hard and became an assistant manager of a fast food restaurant I had begun as a fry cook to kill time before boot camp, tried to be a wife, failed at being a wife, and later got a job as an insurance rep, then a vet tech, working nights bartending and provided for my child until she left home, came back, left home again finally and here I am in my late forties, worn out physically and settled in to my very loving life with Dan. I couldn't get into the military if I wanted too, but I do not want those goals anymore. My chance has passed and I am very satisfied with what I do every day saving wildlife.

I pulled myself out of the choices I made by *the skin of my teeth*. I had strong work ethics that carried me through, but I once worked three jobs to support my child and I know what it feels like to work 20 hours a day for months at a time. It is nothing short of hell.

I do not regret having my child. Very few people regret their children, but I regret losing track of the plan for my own future. I was lucky. I wound up with a lifetime career doing what I love, but financial stability and the benefits of a career were lost forever. Trust me. A child is not a tragedy, but a child is trading one set of goals for another altogether.

You are in control of what you do behind closed doors with another person. Be careful. It can change your life forever.

CHAPTER 3
"EMPLOYMENT. GET SOME"

Hopefully your parents have required you to experience some sort of employment over the years preparing you for adulting. Whether it was babysitting or mowing lawns, you performed a service in exchange for money. That is basically the rest of your life as a working adult providing for yourself and someday maybe a family.

Your employment habits are crucial to your future work history and those habits will follow you forever. Read on to learn some valuable advice when embarking on life as an employee. It will help you tremendously.

CREATING YOUR JOB HISTORY-
Employment records are like a road map of your past. Future employers will someday be reading your work history on your job application. You will want to make sure that all your time after the age of eighteen is accounted for, and any jobs prior to adulthood contain satisfactory references if that is all you have. They WILL contact your

previous employers and verify dates and basic work habits. Protect your freedom to be honest and open about those dates. Any lengthy gaps in time will be assumed to be employment you do not wish to disclose, and those gaps are alarming to a potential employer. "*What are they hiding? WHAT DID THEY DO WRONG?*" is often the assumption. If you have any legitimate gaps in your work history, account for them on the application and *explain* them. "Worked six months for a mission in Haiti" "Moved in with Grandmother to assist her" "Had surgery with lengthy recovery"
You get the idea. Account for your time and take the mystery out of your history. It will make a difference.

When you land a job, make sure it is something you truly intend to do long term. Multiple short term jobs will deem you unstable, and employers will be reluctant to invest the funds in your training. You have to realize that until you are properly trained to be productive in any job, you are an *investment of their resources*. They pay you to learn and they pay others to teach you. All they have to go by to take you on is your work history. You need to present yourself as a good investment based on your track record.

If you find yourself in a job that you realize you want/need to leave, do it *properly*. Give notice to your employer. This is not the time to vent. This is a time to negotiate. Let them know with plenty of advance notice that you are going to be leaving. Give them a specific date of at least two to four weeks in the future. Many employers will choose to let you go sooner. That is their option. *"Short timer's disease"* is when an employee is working their notice and is less productive, sometimes careless, and often is contagious to other staff as short time employees spread their *"escape plan"* epiphany, inspiring others to follow suit. Many employers would prefer to avoid this period of concern and end your employment at the time of notice, so *BE PREPARED* for that.

If you are starting a new job that is waiting for you to work your notice at a former job, make sure you have the funds saved to compensate or the option to begin your new job immediately. Either way, you need to be flexible, professional and prepared to accept the transition between jobs if things fall outside of your control. The way you handle yourself to your former employer will determine how they are listed on future applications that may haunt you for your entire job hunting life. It is frustrating to leave gaps in your future applications because things ended badly. Part of being an adult is considering how your choices affect others, and what the consequences might be for you. This company hired you once upon a time. They took a chance on you, they invested training in you. Don't make them regret it.

DRESS FOR THE JOB YOU WANT, NOT THE JOB YOU'RE APPLYING FOR- Yes, we have all been raised by the adage; *"Don't judge a book by its cover"* and we are all aware of laws against discrimination based on all sorts of factors, *however* like it or not we are all silently judged by our own personal presentation.

If you show up to a job interview in your casual worst, that is how they will perceive your future efforts as an employee. You are saying *"I don't care enough about this interview to try".* If you are going to put forth the time an effort to try for a job, any job, you may as well mean it. You can have a stunning resume, loads of education and look amazing on paper, and blow it in the first impression before you even open your mouth. *"But I want to be hired for my abilities, not my appearance!"*

Sounds perfect, and in a perfect world that would be the case, but you have to understand that your appearance is the wrapper that the package comes in, and human nature dictates that we all believe the most attractive wrappers contain the best gifts!

Ladies, *sex does not sell* in an interview so please button it up, look professional and don't give the impression that you may be a target for sexual harassment on the job. No employer wants to deal with the distraction and drama of your need for attention. You are far more than your looks. Get attention with your brilliant personality and work ethics. Getting sexual attention might feel good, but when that is all you become to the people around you, it will eat at your self-esteem and you will have to work harder to eliminate the image you have created for yourself.

AVOID RELATIONSHIPS IN THE WORKPLACE- Here is a slippery slope for you! Though having a love interest conveniently located at your place of employment might be fun and exciting, you have to realize that there is a very strong possibility that this person who will now know you better than anyone else in the workplace, and possibly intimately, may very well someday turn on you or hurt you. All that the two of you have shared could one day become *work place gossip fodder*. It is hard to go to work every day and maintain focus on your job while people are whispering behind your back, and spreading intimate details about you. It is even more difficult to consolidate facing on a daily basis, someone who has hurt you and being forced to communicate with them. It also does not bode well to your employer. They will avoid putting you in a position of responsibility and management if you cannot maintain a professional relationship with other staff. Realize that everything you choose to do at work creates either a reward or consequence for your future, and leaving a job because you messed up and dated a co-worker who made life unbearable for you just devalues your work history. Avoid creating the problem in the first place. Make friends at work. People you count on. People who have your back. People who support your missions and goals, and avoid destroying those friendships by turning them into relationships. It's far too risky and can destroy everything you have worked for.

CHAPTER 4
"The Legal System. Friend or Foe?"

If you are launching into adulthood and at any point you are visited by flashy red and blue lights causing you to have the sudden feeling of utter fear and horror, *YOU ARE DOING IT WRONG!* A judge does not care that your girlfriend/boyfriend cheated on you and you went on a drinking binge, or had a fight in your front yard. A judge does not care that your 'designated driver' flaked on you and left the party early. A judge does not care that your BFF hid their weed in your glove box and you were unaware. A judge does not care that your mom texted you while you were driving and she gets cranky if you don't respond. A judge does not care *WHY* you did what you did. The judge has one concern and one concern only; that you learn your lesson before anyone gets hurt, and that you never ever want to be in front of their court again.

$10,000. Big number. What could you do with *TEN THOUSAND DOLLARS?* Lots of stuff I would imagine. That's a sweet trip to some really cool place for a month or more, a cruise for two with all the extras, a better car, a year's rent in some places. It's college tuition for a while, or paying your parents back for all the loans, or the gaming system of your dreams twice! It is also about the price of being caught *"driving under the influence"* of drugs or alcohol. Imagine paying that to a lawyer, restitution to any victims or fines and fees at the court house, and that is getting off cheap and easy if you didn't maim or kill someone in the process of your stupid choice to drive under the influence or answer a text from behind the wheel. That possibility could end your freedom for *the REST of your LIFE*. "Voluntary manslaughter" is a charge that absolutely could rid you of the need to make another decision for yourself forever. A vehicle under the control of someone who is not competent or responsible in controlling it is considered a weapon to do harm. Take this possibility seriously from the *beginning* of your life and make safe operation of a vehicle a line you never cross, you never fudge, or

make excuses for. Use taxis or ride shares, or even call your parents. They may not be happy to get up in the night and come get you, or thrilled with you for putting yourself in the situation, but they will be comforted that you made an adult choice in the end and made sure you got yourself *(and everyone else on the road)* home safely.

You do not have to be drunk to be careless and kill someone or yourself from behind the wheel of a vehicle. There are parents out there today trying to consolidate the loss of their child and move forward without the desire to end their own life because their child was a distracted driver. *You know all of this, you have heard all of this* and my hope and your parents hope is that it all scared you enough to prevent you from texting while driving, but if you are still doing it, stop. *Just stop.* You are not yet an experienced enough driver to get away with distractions. You might get away with it once or even a thousand times, and the next time you and a handful of people and your best friend riding shotgun in your car are all listed in the "Area Deaths" section of your local paper, fighting for real estate in the local cemetery, and your little miracle of existence on the tiny rock spinning through infinite space, being warmed by the star with a shelf life, *IS OVER*. Nonmatter what your beliefs are for an afterlife, let's just say for the sake of argument that *this* is the fun place. *Stick around awhile.* The world needs you or you wouldn't be here.

CHAPTER 5
"Money Matters Because Money Matters"

DO NOT LOSE TRACK OF THE PLAN- Many young adults leave home with all sorts of plans for their future and are easily side tracked by the reality (and hardship) of freedom and independence, and never really quite find their way back to the plan. Even if your *"job of less desire"* takes up most of your time, and your motivation to work on your future goals becomes less motivating, just imagine life as it is now, *FOREVER.* You are the only person who can create change for yourself, and only you can step up on your behalf and do the work to improve your future. If you are satisfied with *"this is all I can handle"* and *"I don't need financial security, retirement or vacations"* then so be it, but trust me here; *life will continue to pile things on you, not take them away.* As time marches on, things will become harder to change, not easier. The younger you are, the easier you bounce back from stress and pressure, and the less adult obstacles will lay in your way, so make time every day to apply to your future goals so you are never complacent to accept less than you are capable of achieving.

Many of those *'older people'* going to school are people who left their path long ago and got side tracked with dead end jobs, having children, supporting a spouse (*who may have left them after they walked away from their careers to support their spouse's aspirations and build a family*) or spent nearly a lifetime of regret for abandoning their goals. They are finally over the humps in time that got between themselves and *"what do I want to be when I grow up"* and are finally back on track in the latter part of their lives, trying to salvage their chance. Many of them don't even *need* to follow through now, they just want to end the cycle of regret and *'what ifs'*. Don't make the same mistakes they did. Stay on track while you have the option and ability now. Your life will never be more in your control than it is right now, no matter what you believe or how supported you may be. Stick to the plan and if that doesn't work out, form another plan. Don't be without a plan.

Your life will forever be built on the foundation you create over the next five to ten years.

DON'T GET SUCKED INTO HYPE- There is a whole WORLD filled with vultures just lying in wait for naive, young adults with undamaged credit histories and no clue. Before my daughter was old enough to read the $5,000 set of encyclopedias that I bought for her when she was a baby, we had Google. I had fire alarms throughout my house at the cost of thousands when a $5 smoke detector worked better. I believed that part of being a responsible adult was to buy into the fear mongers who visited my home and sold me item after item to "better my future and keep me and mine safe". Today the onslaught is mainly internet based, but it is all the same. *YOU ARE IN DANGER OF MANIPULATION.* Realize it, accept it and know that you are *ideal* prey for those who are predatory on your finances. Before making any financial commitments, always get an outside opinion. Accept that you are not yet experienced in all things contractual and when you sign on the bottom line with any commitment, you OWE

IT no matter what you get for your money. Sure contracts can be overturned within a court, but it is hard to do and it will be expensive. You can't possibly know it all. Accept it. Get direction, which brings me to;

DO NOT IGNORE YOUR CREDIT SCORE- Your credit score may not seem important to you now, but just like the road map that is your work history and your "I used to be stupid but I'm not anymore.. *trust me*" criminal record, your credit history will be used to extort money from your pocket *FOR THE REST OF YOUR LIFE*. Protect your credit score by paying cash whenever possible, financing the least amount you can get away with and negotiate for better terms on anything you do finance. Some day you will want to buy a house. Your mortgage may be the largest financial investment of your entire life. Rent is fine, but those funds go into someone else's pocket. Buying a home is like a savings account, but your interest rate determines how much of the money you pay goes into your pocket (equity) or is profit for the bank (interest). They charge you to loan you that money over decades, and the profit they make is decided by the risk of the loan. (Your credit score and history). Protecting your credit score now, will determine how much you have to pay to borrow money later. Every time you apply for a credit card, are late on a payment, run a credit check, leave a bill unpaid, or finance something, your credit score is negatively affected. The best way to navigate through your financial life is to use debit cards whenever possible, stick with the same bank, open a savings account and put something in it each week or month for emergencies, budget your fun and spending money, refrain from luxury items, adopt practical shopping methods, avoid gifts and loans to friends, pay your bills FIRST, do not co-sign a loan for anyone, and any credit card you use to get by, PAY IT OFF as soon as possible. Do not let the balance build up. Your financial goal should be to have an 800+ credit score before you ever LOOK at a house to purchase. It is possible and it will save you tens of thousands of dollars over the lifetime of your mortgage, and put more of your own money back into your pocket when and if you sell.

TIPS FOR CAR SHOPPING- Cars can be a huge trap into getting in over your head on payments. So many lenders are competing for your money that loans are made that consumers cannot really afford. There are many honest dealerships out there that will help you to buy only what you can afford, but beware of the "you can easily afford this" speech, the "variable interest rate" which is a killer, or any form of "balloon payment". These are all financial traps for you later on. Calculate your budget before shopping for a car and if the dealer cannot meet your needs, walk away. They will keep you there for hours just to give you a price and payment terms. It is all part of the manipulation so you will have your time invested and your hopes high. They count on you to take whatever deal they offer just to get out of there dealership with a new car after spending half a day waiting for someone to tell you the bottom line. Don't fall for it. Stand your ground. It is *your* money you are spending after all, and if you have a salesman that has a sob story of how he will be fired if he doesn't make a sale today, *MOVE ON!* I was sucked into that one when I was your age. I was a compassionate kid and he had a dozen photos of his children all over his desk. Years later I was in the same office with the same photos, different salesman! *Buyer beware.*

The best way to shop for a car is pre approval through your own bank, and walk on the car lot with your financing terms ready and look at lots where the prices are posted clearly on the car. Never let them know how much you can spend, and always try to negotiate. Most dealers will, and always have a trusted mechanic or vehicle savvy friend of your own choosing look over any used car prior to purchase. There is a lot of cover up and polish that goes into a lemon to distract you from the problems that can cost you thousands later on. Get someone to bring those issues to light before you commit to ownership.

CHAPTER 6
"So far this all sounds like work. What's fun now?"

Oh don't worry. There are lots of fun things for you to do now. You have no idea who you are yet and even though you are making that face at us for taking all the fun out of adulting, you will someday realize how right we are about everything, even if it doesn't apply to you directly.

Finding your identity in this world is an adventure that you may not realize you are having. You may begin your adult life as one person, and one day years down the road, feel like you have just met yourself for the first time. It happened for me at age 27. I was lucky. For some it can take decades, or even tragically, *never happen for them.*

The key to figuring out who you are in the world begins by being open to new experiences and trying new things. You never know what might fit, so don't be afraid to adventure and add to your list of *"things I have done"*. A 'bucket list' is a list of experiences that people save to one day do before they die. Your goal should be to make sure that list is very short when you are older and life becomes packed with responsibility, and take the time for yourself now before you make a family and take on a mortgage and become obligated to a career that you work without fail to retirement.

Some people view this time as *"nose to the grindstone, make my parents proud"* and others see "Party time! Excellent!" and all is a blur until they wake up and rake up the pieces and start again. Either way, nothing is stopping you from testing the waters of any new adventure at any given time.

Volunteering is the BEST way to experience all sorts of valuable journeys without the obligation of a job. Granted, you may not have the free time to give away, but if you look at that time the same way you look at an internship, then you will see that it is an investment in experience, and not necessarily something you lose.

If you are someone like me who loves the company of animals, look into volunteering at a zoo, animal shelter or rescue group. If you enjoy helping people, find a soup kitchen, church group, nursing home, or homeless mission. If you enjoy mentoring children there are many worthy organizations where you can be of use.

Volunteering not only helps you grow as a person and assists you in self-discovery and possibly enlightening you to alternative paths in life where you will be more fulfilled, but it also looks *very good on your resume.* Employers will view you for your volunteer time as someone who will go the extra mile for their community, and that person will likely go the extra mile for their company as well. It builds character and skills that will follow you for a lifetime.

I began volunteering as a youth. At 13 years old I was teaching children with physical challenges to trick ride horses. The rewards I gained from that time stuck with me. Every job I have had since has utilized the communication skills I learned when I patiently explained to those awesome children how to sit a horse and be safe. I have been in charge of people at nearly every job since and managed huge responsibility to keep people safe and informed. You never know where the jewels of wisdom during your lifetime will come from. Be open to search for them.

CHAPTER 7
"Parents don't want to *have to* parent anymore"

Hard to believe but it is true. Weather you have "Velcro parents" who stick to you and don't want to let go, or the *"Oh my God are you still here??"* parents who turned your bedroom into a home office before your boxes of stuff made it to the front porch, they really are ready to stop worrying about your welfare. It is a hard habit to break to be concerned about the daily life of another person every day for 18+ years and then suddenly, due to the turning of a calendar page, *ITS OVER*. We hate to see it all end, and more than that, we worry about your safety and have to accept not being able to protect you from the big bad evil world, but the truth of the matter is that is has all been quite *exhausting.* All 'empty nesters' are trying to remember what they enjoyed doing before the babies came into their lives and figure out what to do with all the leftover concern they have every day. Sometimes we fumble around for it and wind up parenting you out of sheer boredom or force of habit. We don't mean to encroach on your freedom and independence, we just can't seem to stop feeling like you can't survive without us!

The best way we can break the chains or cut the apron strings and stop considering you in every step we take is to literally stop making your life our constant concern. Most parents struggle and will call you for every reason from "Did you pay your tuition?" to "Are you wearing clean *underwear?*" and then when you really need something, they act like you are a huge intrusion into their lives and a leach on their resources. What it up with that?

I know, sounds harsh doesn't it? Well it's sort of like this;
You get this dog. The dog is your responsibility. You feed the dog, you bathe the dog, you take it to the vet, you get it fixed, and you get it vaccinated. You accept everything you have to do to care for this dog and keep it alive because it is your

responsibility and you love it. Then one day the dog runs away. It finds a new home with new people and lives for many years with its new family, forgetting you ever existed, but you can't stop thinking about your long lost dog, wondering what happened to it, imagining the worst.

Years go by and the people find your old tattered "lost dog" sign and return your dog, along with the bills for all its care (which you resist paying because you haven't had the benefit of the dog) AND the dog no longer listens to you or loves you, it resents that it is in your care and only wants to leave again, but it is still YOUR dog! You love your dog, but this is some mutant version of your dog that no longer needs you or wants you but the obligations are still the same. You now struggle to accept your dog. You secretly wish he would run away again.

Being a parent of a child who has grown up and left home is a lot like that. It is a begrudging non-responsibility that we will gripe and moan about after we have served our parenting years fully responsible but now have the legal option to decline a request for care, but out of fear of *"if not me than who?"* we are there for you. We love you, so we will continue to support whatever makes sense to us, and keep you off the streets and fed, but we will always be far more willing to give than to be asked of, and let's face it, you all come back to us resenting us for your needing us, and that is not fair, but it *is normal.*

If you want your parents help, *deserve it*. That's all we ask! It is so simple and such a basic rule in adulting. If we feel extorted as parents, and feel drug back into an obligation we have fulfilled, we may begin to resent it and that will directly affect how we feel about helping and if we choose to help at all. Parenting an adult child who is independent, happy with themselves, has their life together and knows who they are and what they want in the world is an ABSOLUTE JOY! I have one of those, but it wasn't easy to get her there! *"People kept bringing my dog back!"* So far this last move out to the big bad world is sticking, but it is based on a relationship. I turned her bedroom into a game room for my husband's son, but I bought a new comfy couch just in case. *I AM AN ENABLER IN DENIAL*. Got it? Good.

The bottom line is this; cultivate a good adult relationship with your parents, be appreciative and deserving of any help they provide, avoid asking for help until you have turned every stone to solve your own problems, and if they judge you fairly, *own it and change it*. If it is unfair, prove them wrong. Their opinion of you is probably very close to correct, and if it's not, show them who you are. If the entire rest of the world turns their back on you, your family will still be there. Make sure they are willing if the time comes.

Chapter 8
"Mind your social media footprints"

Today more than ever before, employers, potential partners, college administration, family members and law enforcement have the tools to discover your character from any cell phone or personal computer. Social media may be an outlet for everything interesting or entertaining that you do, but it is also a trap for your past to affect your future, and there are people who today might be considered trusted friends who one day might turn against you and wield whatever ammunition you have allowed to be recorded in the great abyss that is the internet against you.

Imagine every photo ever uploaded, every text or comment, every party all night video or stupid thing you've ever done, being viewed by your children someday. Try telling your teenager that drinking and drugs are bad and then having them face you with photos of you doing exactly that once upon a time! It is hard for hypocrites to parent effectively.

I know that now seems like the only time in your life that matters. Your brain is still maturing and consequences do not seem like something that will affect you years down the road, *but they will*. People who are trying to decide who you are do not separate the 'old you' from the 'new and improved adult you'. They are looking up your history to form an opinion of you and whatever they find will be forever attached to that opinion. You will be judged silently and not even realize it at times. That job you applied for that you were overqualified for that never even resulted in an interview might have been lost by the wayside because of the photos you posted on spring break at the beer pong-strip poker marathon where you lost miserably and wound up naked on a pool floaty. It can happen! It *does* happen!

Mind your social media footprint and your recorded behavior. The best advice I can give you is since everyone is walking around with a video camera in their hands, avoid situations that can compromise your image altogether. Part of being an adult is to protect your reputation and avoid damaging your future. Think about what you post yourself and the way you regard others on social media. How you handle problems and voice your opinion is also a tell-tale sign of your character. It all matters. "Freedom of speech" is a great freedom to have, but others are also free to form their opinions of you for it.

Chapter 9
"People are people"

Equality and Co-existence. Hopefully you were raised with the values that people are people and so long as other people mean you no harm, they have the same right to be here and have access to the same opportunities as you.

The population of our world is made up of a wide variety of colors, beliefs, traditions, histories and priorities. People are all a product of their environment and rearing. Your back story will be similar to most of the people that you spend time with, and once in a while you will meet someone with a completely different set of beliefs and lifestyle. You will be amazed at some of the differences, and you might even be made uncomfortable as your own core beliefs will contradict the things that others hold most true. *It's okay*. They are not infectious. The easiest way to be in the world is to realize that *"everyone has their own truth"*, which is something my mother said to me every time I was offended or confused by the behavior of another. Every person you see has a back story that you may know nothing about. Many people have suffered abuse, neglect or hardships that you could not possibly relate too, and be glad for it if that is the case, and if it isn't, realize you are far from alone in the world for your struggles.

The worst thing you could do to someone who is suffering in silence is to judge them without knowing their history, their struggles or their obstacles in life.

My mother-in-law who I love as my *'bonus mom'*, is a brilliant, giving woman. She doesn't like to get upset with people so she makes up her own back stories for people who offend her so that she can be instantly understanding and forgiving rather than angry. When someone is rude to her in the store, she tells herself *"She just found out her mother has cancer and she is upset"* or the man who cuts her off in traffic and speeds past her, she says to herself *"His wife was just in a car accident and he is trying to get to her."*

She recently told me about that exact scenario. As the car cut her off and sped past, she excused him so he could get to his 'wife's side'. A few miles ahead she caught up to the same car who was pulled over on the roadside at the scene of an accident, assisting medics as they loaded a woman from the wreck into an ambulance.

It gave me chills when she told the story.

It just goes to show you that you never know what is affecting someone else, and unless they are causing harm to you or others, try to be patient with people. After all, people are just merely human. Imperfect, flawed, self-absorbed at times and often thoughtless, and we may never ever understand why, and that's okay too. But if you come across a situation where someone else or yourself is being victimized for their difference in race, beliefs or otherwise, do everything you can to put a stop to it. Be a hero in this world without putting yourself in danger. Complacency toward abuse is a disease in our culture. Don't spend one moment ashamed for not helping someone else escape a bully. Be a voice for the benefit of any victim you encounter be it human or animal.

We all have a right to be treated with respect as a living, feeling creature, and the future of the way we all exist in the world is truly in your hands. Take it seriously.

CHAPTER 10
"Change is part of the journey"

When time marches by and life sends you out into the big, wide world, be prepared for change. Be prepared for *lots* of change. For example, many parents no longer need the big two story house once their children have flown the nest and suddenly the house is up for sale so your college can be paid for and mom and dad can preserve their retirement fund for retirement fun. *Feel guilty? Don't!* This is just one example of *life moving on* and it is all part of the process of raising a family and then being done, and rewarding themselves with less responsibility and fewer financial obligations.

Your high school friends that you swore you would continue to hang out with every single weekend after graduation, may soon seem scattered to the wind and no longer available for any nostalgic fun. Some will find themselves immediately committed with unplanned children on the way, and their priorities will shift instantly. Your friendship may be painfully ignored and their world will become filled by the people they depend on to help support them. Jobs will transfer people far away from you and universities will create long distance friends who share every moment with you until they meet new people to take your place in their lives.

What I am trying to express to you is this process of monumental loss after you walk across the stage and graduate into adulting is *normal*. Be grateful for the home you grew up in, the friends who carried you through your school years, and the memories and bonds you forged as your lives marched parallel together. You will always treasure them, and now it is time for a new adventure, and letting the old life go is part of finding a new one.

Listen when I tell you that if you make it through life with even *one* friend that was with you in the beginning and is still with you at the end, you are very blessed and even unique. Your friends are not the only ones who will change and grow and abandon the friendships that once were sacred and replace those with new people and priorities. You will too.

CHAPTER 11
"Good advice to take with you"

*Religious based beliefs will help you grow in strength and conviction, but you do not have to be religious to have beliefs. Make a list of five or more beliefs that you wish to live by, and hold strong to them. We are guided and protected by our beliefs and convictions. If you don't have any, you need to find some. They will help define who you are in this world.

*File taxes each year by mid April. Yes, you can file early. Make sure you have all your w-2 forms from all employers. Don't ignore taxes. Sooner or later it will all catch up to you.

*Life is a brief moment in time. You are existing on a chunk of minerals spinning in space, being heated by a star that has a shelf life, in an infinite universe that we are barely able to understand or describe. The human race's entire existence is insignificant in the bigger picture of the universe. Your very life is a tiny and precious miracle in time and space. Know it and act like it. Don't waste it.

*Never put anyone on your mobile phone plan unless you are married. You will eventually regret it. We all do.

*Objects are objects. You can love your car, but it will never love you back. You can save for months for that designer bag, but it will not solve your problems. Before you spend, ask yourself *"Will this purchase enhance or hamper my peace of mind?"* You will find that having money when you need it is far more important than having the things you want.

*Never loan money to a friend unless you are prepared to never see your friend or your money again. A 'gift' will only cost you money, and a friend that repays a gift is worthy of your friendship and trust.

*Good looks disappear over time. Inner beauty is easier to maintain and lasts forever.

Be sure you are always attractive on the inside.

*People will judge you by the company you keep. Select friends who are ahead of you in life rather than behind you. You will catch up rather than be held back.

*Parents know when you are wasting your money. They typically won't say anything without proof, but trust me, the hand outs will get smaller and smaller until you figure out what you're doing wrong.

*In any love interest relationship remember; you are responsible for the situations you get yourself into. Be very careful of who you commit too, share secrets with and share a roof with. Don't risk your companion becoming your captor. There are people who will control you with your innermost secrets. Be careful who you share them with.

*Your car tags are due every year. Yes, really!

*Car insurance is a legal necessity, not an option. You might hate paying for it but if you ever need it and do not have it, you will regret it.

*Loving yourself is something we all need to learn to do before we can forge healthy, successful relationships. It is impossible to fully receive love if you don't believe you are worthy, and people will only treat you as well as you require. Set your own standards of the treatment you require to stay in a relationship or others soon will.

*Music and exercise will elevate your mood. It is legal and non-fattening. Opt for music and/or exercise instead of being an emotional eater or turning to substances to feel better. We all have days when we don't like ourselves. Do something healthy about it.

*When someone says nasty things about you, rise above it. Do not retaliate with the same loathing and venom. You are truly no better than they are if you do.

*Taking that of which is not yours makes you a thief. Thieves steal more than objects and money. They rob others of their feeling of security and control in the world. Don't be a thief. Thieves suck.

*When someone wise is speaking, shut up and listen. It is free education.

*Just because you read it on the internet does not make it true.

*Illegal drugs and alcohol are poor choices and will never be anything other than poor choices. They often lead to addiction. Addiction is a force of need that you cannot control. It takes over your life, robs you of your priorities and destroys who you are. The greatest lie you will ever hear is "Take this. You will feel better. It won't hurt you." Remember, *it is all poison* and an addict is typically the last person to figure out they *are* one.

*Try using a road map once in a while instead of your GPS. You become more capable, safe and independent if you can find your way in the world without technology.

*Friends will come and go. Relationships will end and life will send you reeling again and again in agony over the cruelty and injustice of others. Know that the damage they create is often from damage done to them. Don't be another casualty in this world. Keep your heart open and always believe in the good in your own heart and others.

*Forgiveness is the key to peace. Always. That doesn't mean you give people who have wronged you a free pass. You learn from your journey, let go of anger and move forward.

*Never miss an opportunity to enhance someone's day. You get from the world what you give. It costs you nothing to be polite, thoughtful and above all, pleasant to be around.

*Don't sweat the petty things and don't pet the sweaty things.

*We all suffer the same. Have compassion for anyone who seems to be struggling. You do not know what is behind their pain. Not everyone shares the horrors of their reality.

*Before reacting to a confrontation or offense, think twice about how you respond. Never hit "send" or "post" in anger. Always calm down so you can think clearly about how your words can be used against you or misconstrued, and apologies do not repair the broken pieces of another's heart, but healing only begins with *"I'm sorry"*.

* The weather is always a safe topic of conversation with people you do not trust.

*Whenever you bend to assist the smallest of need, you stand taller than those who walk past.

*Children should never be brought into the world to fulfill you. Your job will always and only be to fulfill a child. They are not an accessory to your life but will become your life. Wait until you are ready.

*Lights that come on in the dash of your car are not for decoration. When a new light comes on, take it to a mechanic. Oil needs changed every 3,000 miles or so. Yes, really!

*Eat healthy, take care of your teeth, don't poison your body with things that you do not need. You only have one body for the rest of your life. As you age, all that you do to abuse and neglect yourself now will come back to haunt you later.

*If you make a mistake, OWN IT! If you do the wrong thing, ADMIT IT! Accountability is part of maturity and you cannot be considered an adult if you do not take responsibility for your actions. Excuses make us look weak, entitled, untrustworthy and immature. People who own up to a mistake, are learning from them. People who make excuses are avoiding responsibility. Which do think an employer would prefer on their team?

*Once you turn eighteen, no one owes you anything. Entitlement is the belief that you are owed something that you have not earned. Whining about the promotion you felt you were cheated out of our the raise you didn't get will only confirm to the rest of the world that you are too immature to deserve whatever it is you think is yours. Earn your way and when things don't pan out the way you hope, try harder, negotiate for it or do something else. Though your work record is important, you are not held captive in any job. If you feel you are being treated unfairly in life, change the plan, but realize that you are your own priority and often your contributions will be overlooked. Sooner or later, we all get recognized for loyalty, commitment and dedication, which is far better than being known for complaints.

*If your life goes in the proper order, you will outlive your parents. You will never stop needing them no matter how well you do on your own. Make sure they know that and you will have no regrets when they are gone. And above all else, don't take yourself and your relationships at this time in your life too seriously. People will come and go and your heart will be broken again and again. It is all part of the journey to mature and learn to navigate through the future and find your place in the world. Though a situation might feel crushing and critical, in the scheme of the rest of your life it will simply be an experience you learned from that grew you into a much stronger and wiser adult.

*If you are fortunate enough to earn a living doing something you are passionate about, you have succeeded. Money will never buy you happiness. Feeling good about what you do to get it always will.

*Facial piercings, implants and tattoos can be individual statements of your creative freedom OR look really really stupid when you are interviewing for a job in your forties. Before committing to a body modification, make sure you can live with it now and later on. You will see when you are my age and your friends are suffering through tattoo removals and earlobe reconstruction, and explaining their obscenely depicted 'tramp stamp' to their teenagers. Your life will likely change, but ink lasts until you can afford laser surgery.
If you have to have a name inked into your skin, the only names you should ever put on your body need to be your parents or your

children, or a tribute to someone who has passed. Period. Branding yourself doesn't make anyone stay.

What we take with us from each hardship or mistake is not meant to traumatize us or hamper our development, but to give us the tools and skills to reflect on our past to consolidate and navigate our future. Your perspective when going through rough experiences will help you to learn the important lessons and avoid emotional damage. We all experience traumatic pain and fear in our lives and we all somehow survive to smile and laugh once again. No period of darkness is forever unless you allow it. You have so many options in this world and as time goes by, they will unfold one by one and you will make choices that will change your path forever. Know that any dark place is within your power to shed light. You are not helpless and you are not a victim unless you allow abuse to continue, or choose to live your life as a victim and not get help. You *always* have a choice.

Keep yourself safe and your loved ones in touch and make sure you dedicate time to stay connected to the things you love to do. At the end of it all it is not our possessions and accomplishments that define who we were and the life that we led, but the way others felt about us, the people we lifted along the way and the love that we gave to others. Keep your focus on what will bring you joy, and if your parents are proud, then you know that you turned out okay, and thank them for all the work it took to get you to this point.

Good luck to you. Now go ROCK THIS LIFE!

Annette & Dan

Made in the USA
Columbia, SC
03 August 2021